The Friend Economy

By Roch Tranel

Copyright © 2018 Roch Tranel
All rights reserved.
ISBN-13: 978-1984206640
ISBN-10: 1984206648
Printed by CreateSpace Independent
Publishing Platform

Here's What's Inside...

5   **Introduction**

7   **The Friend Economy**

8   **Why More Business Owners Don't Tap Into The Friend Economy**

9   **How to Attract Business by Being More Clear About Who You Are**

10   **Build Good Relationships with People Who Have Similar Values**

12   **What Are the Key Mindshifts to Make to Be Successful with The Friend Economy**

17   **How Using The Friend Economy Means You Don't Have to Worry About Losing Clients**

18   **The Friend Economy Works for All Personality Types**

19   **Don't Focus on Yourself, Focus on Your Clients**

20   **Mistakes to Avoid While Building Your Friend Economy**

24 **The Paradox: It's Easier to Engage with Your Clients as a Friend than as a Business Acquaintance**

26 **Here's How to Get Started on Your Friend Economy**

29 **Why Your Clients Are Happier When They Have a Friend Economy**

31 **How to Join and Be a Part of Roch's Friend Economy**

35 **Here's How to Build an Abundant Business Powered by a Community of Friends**

37 **About the Author**

Introduction

The Friend Economy

I think there is a movement underway in business. The transparency of social media means we have to be our true selves as a business and no longer rely on "selling stuff." Today, relationships rule, and building friendships is what business is all about.

One thing people often ask me is, why doesn't the usual business woes affect my business? The answer I believe, is people are looking for deeper relationships with everyone around them, and because I know who I am, I am not shy about sharing my philosophy on life with those around me. This transparency allows everyone, including customers and business associates to clearly see what I am all about. I believe this makes me more approachable and able to attract more people into my community.

You see, unlike most business owners, I call my clients friends, and as a result my business grows even when the economy is struggling. Friends stay longer than clients—it's that simple. My business is not based on a fickle, ever-changing marketing platform where people seem more and more disengaged. Instead I invest my time in getting to know and become friends with my clients, which is the foundation of **The Friend Economy**.

This book is the result of wanting to show other business owners how to build a thriving and successful business. It will help them build a community of people who want to do business with them, thereby helping them succeed.

What follows is the transcript where I share with you why I think building your own **Friend Economy** is the right way to ensure that your business is both engaging and thriving. I hope these pages encourage you to reach out and build lifelong partnerships with people who care about you (as much as you care about them) and create a wonderful, fruitful business together.

Enjoy the book!

Your Friend,

Roch Tranel

The Friend Economy

Susan: Good morning, this is Susan Austin, and with me today is Roch Tranel from Libertyville, Illinois. Welcome Roch.

Roch: Thank you very much. It's good to be on the call with you, Susan.

Susan: We're here to talk about your book *The Friend Economy*. What is The Friend Economy?

Roch: I am excited to talk about The Friend Economy because I believe after the economy crashed in 2008, the world changed. Business owners are struggling to figure out how to do business in today's new economy. Things are not working as easy as before the economy crashed. Business owners are concerned about where the next wave of business is going to come from. They have a staff to keep employed and systems to maintain. These things keep them up at night. The Friend Economy is about tapping into the community of people who already know and like you, while successfully doing business with them. I believe they want to do business with you because of their respect for you. Business owners aren't tapping into this community, and when they do they'll find it's very beneficial for both them and their community. They want peace of mind that things are going to be okay.

I am suggesting business owners have a group of people who know, trust, and respect them already. These include friends, neighbors, parents of their kids' friends who they see at sporting events and at church every week...just a few examples. They are friends with these people, but they don't know how to bridge the gap and approach them about what it is they do. They don't know how to tap into the business realm of their friends in order to help them grow their business and at the same time, still maintain a friendship.

The Friend Economy is how to bridge the gap and turn friends into clients. The Friend Economy is building a community of people with whom you do business with and not just to be friends with. These people already know and like you. I believe they want to do business with you because they already have a great deal of respect for you. Business owners just aren't tapping into this community, which is right in front of them, and when they do, they will find it's very beneficial for both their business and their community.

Why More Business Owners Don't Tap Into The Friend Economy

Susan: Why do you suppose this is? What gets in the way of a business owner reaching out to their friends?

Roch: I think people are afraid to put themselves "out there." You have to be really clear about who you are and what you stand for. I'm not sure people actually realize who they are, what they stand for, and what their values are. As a part of this book, I want to encourage people to put a stake in the ground and say, "This is who I am. This is what I am all about. I am not ashamed of anything." I suggest they share this excitement with their friends, and if they are encouraged and energized by what you are up to, they will be fired up and want to be a part of it as well.

Enthusiasm is contagious and both parties benefit from someone being passionate. When you are really passionate about what you do and you know you are having a positive impact on the world, you want the people who are closest to you to be the most impacted.

I am suggesting business owners should bridge this relationship between the people they already know and start engaging with them. And I also encourage them to build a bigger community of people they know and care about, with sincerity in looking forward to helping them.

How to Attract Business by Being More Clear About Who You Are

Susan: A lot of business owners seem to have their business and their personal life separated and you want to remove this separation. Is that what you're saying?

Roch: Yes, I want to remove the separation, because if you're really authentic about who you are, there should not be the business side of you and then the friend side. It should be one and the same person. You shouldn't be somebody at church and somebody different in a board meeting at work. You should be authentic and real no matter who you are engaging. This book will hopefully encourage you to step out and let people see all of who you really are. Ideally they'll be attracted to you and want to be a part of what you are up to - so much so - that they will want to help you grow your business as you help them grow their business too!

Also, it is really important for you to be authentic about who you are. If you are selling life insurance and you are telling people to have the appropriate amount of life insurance, you better have that same life insurance yourself. If you are selling cars or if you are selling a weight loss product or selling a gym membership, you better be working out at that gym; you better be using that same weight loss product. People can tell if you're genuine and authentic. If you are selling Fords you better drive up in a Ford.

Build Good Relationships with People Who Have Similar Values

Susan: Yes, I agree, people can tell if someone is being genuine or if they are putting on a show. You mentioned 2008 when the economy struggled. Why is it important to tap into The Friend Economy since this happened?

Roch: Business owners had an easier time of doing business prior to 2008. Things were all turned upside down, and now business owners have to rethink their business, rethink their cash flow, their revenue; rethink retention of their clients.

People are always looking for the magic bullet for getting and retaining clients. Facebook, social media and LinkedIn are all powerful tools to use in your business. You have to have them today, but I don't think they are the answer to growing your business. I think the answer is building really good relationships with people who have similar values and building this community of friends around you. Friends who like you, who want to do business with you, who want to champion you, who want to see you succeed. This is what The Friend Economy is all about and I believe it is the way to build a successful business going forward.

Susan: You are suggesting Social Media is a tool to support your business versus thinking the tool is the solution?

Roch: Yes, I agree one hundred percent. These tools are a way of connecting with your clients. They are tools to support your Friend Economy because people are busy today. They don't have time to take a 15-minute phone call. But if on Facebook you can let people know what you or your kids or your business is up to, it's a great way for them to stay connected to you. But I don't think it's the answer.

Susan: You mentioned earlier you need to be clear on who you are and what you stand for. Can you elaborate on what you mean by that?

Roch: People have their guard up about letting others know who they really are. They fear somebody may not do business with them because of their ideas, political beliefs or their faith. You cannot worry about what a small amount of people may think about you, because if you do, you're missing out on all the great people who would become attracted to you for standing up for what you believe in.

If you're so worried, Susan, about what people are going to say about you, you don't put anything about you out there. You're not really going to get connected to people and have deep relationships. What you have to say is, I'm going to put myself out there no matter what. If a certain percentage of the population thinks I'm nuts, or they don't agree with my values and refuses to do business with me, you just can't worry about it.

What you have to say is, "This is who I am." I know some people aren't going to like that and will disagree with me. But there are going to be more people who are attracted to what I stand for and I want to connect with them—to become better friends and have them become part of my business economy.

What Are the Key Mindshifts to Make to Be Successful with The Friend Economy

Susan: Very good Roch. What are some of the shifts someone has to make? What would bridge this gap where they are not afraid to put it all out there and say, as you suggested, "This is who I am. This is what I believe in. This is what I'm passionate about."

Roch: I think you have to be comfortable in your own skin and you have to be comfortable letting people know what your faults or deficiencies are. A lot of people don't want to do this because they feel, as a business owner or salesperson, if you're selling cars or selling financial services you have to appear perfect before you can entice someone else to buy your product. I think it's better to be authentic and say, "Look, I'm challenged with this. I've seen the dark side."

One of the shifts you have to make in your thinking is you don't have to be perfect. It's okay to have some flaws and even let those flaws show. I think people really resonate with people whom they view as being authentic and real. They don't want to do business with someone who is too perfect, because when you peel the curtain back, they're like, "Oh, he has some skeletons in his closet." If you are upfront with them and say, "Hey, I didn't do very well at this at a certain time of my life, but I have learned from it and I don't want you to make the same mistakes." Having the mindset of being authentic, being real, and sharing with people some of your faults is a mind shift you have to make to successfully put yourself out there.

In addition to being real and putting yourself out there you have to stand for something. People want to be around people who stand for something. Some people are going to be in your Friend Economy because they agree with what you stand for. Some people are going to be in your Friend Economy because they disagree with what you stand for, but they really respect the fact you are putting yourself out there. Not everyone in your Friend Economy has to agree with you all the time.

What you're doing is saying, "Hey, I stand for something." And for me, Roch Tranel, it's about helping people enjoy a better life. I want to breathe life into everyone I come across. I want to take them from where they are now to some place higher. This could be in regards to their confidence level, finances, career or even a better relationship with their spouse. I have a passion for helping people enjoy a better life. That's the impact I want to have on the world for people who come in contact with me. People who know me know this. It is our company's mantra. I continually have this conversation with people. I've dedicated my life to it.

People know if I am in the room, if I am in the board meeting, there's going to be some contribution I give, which is very positive. I'm not tearing somebody down, but always lifting people up. That's my stake in the ground. That's my massive transformative purpose that I am all about. I think people have to come up with their own massive transformative purpose. Maybe it is about education or crime or injustice or human trafficking. Whatever that happens to be, people need to know what it is about you that is really important to you. What are you really passionate about? Share that with everyone you know and watch what happens.

Susan: You model this quite beautifully, Roch. I've only just met you and your massive transformative purpose is clear to me. There isn't 'work Roch' and 'weekend Roch'.

Roch: Yes, that's absolutely correct. As I said, you can't be one person at work, saying you want to help people enjoy a better life and then come home and not infuse energy and life and passion into your marriage or into your children's lives. People are going to say, "Well, if this is what you're all about, I really want to meet your wife, and I want to see what your kids are all about." They will see for themselves if you are authentic and real in all areas of your life. In church they will notice if you've been the guy that comes early and helps setup; if you're the one who stays late and helps put all the chairs away after the church picnic. Are you really doing what you say you are supposed to be doing?

For me and what I am passionate about; is really a big part of my entire life. I hope this book will encourage people to put those two together. To have one massive transformative purpose regardless of what area of your life it is. People can feel it when you are passionate. They just know it...you don't even have to tell them. You don't have to brag, they simply know what it is you are all about.

Susan: There is an attractiveness to engaging with people like this, isn't there? My guess is because you know what your massive transformative purpose is and so clearly are living it, you do not have to do a lot of hard selling. When you get to this place, you attract people to you and you don't have to convince them of anything. They are attracted to you and want to know more and want to get to know you. Is that right?

Roch: Yes, in fact I recently had a gentleman from Indianapolis, which is a 3-1/2 hour drive, spend a day with me. As we were parting, I asked him what was his biggest insight from the day, thinking it was going to be one of the business strategies he captured from our time together. Instead he said, "I have four or five pages of notes from our meeting. The main thing I wanted to get from you, Roch, was I wanted to be around somebody who is positive and energetic. Yes,

I will go back and implement these strategies, but my cup being filled up was what I came for."

A big part of what makes someone attractive in a very, real authentic way is just being the most positive, inspirational, hopeful person in the room. You give the idea anything is possible, which helps people to realize everything and anything *is* possible.

Susan: I imagine from engaging with people this way your cup is pretty full too.

Roch: That is the cool part about it. In the Friend Economy, when you're encouraging other people, your cup is constantly being filled up by helping them. Your cup, the reader's cup, is going to be filled up when they're naturally authentic and naturally helping people do what they naturally want to do anyway. You are exactly right. When John left that day, I was exhausted, but I was inspired. I was as jazzed up as he was, by helping him and knowing he was going to go back and do some great things with his life.

Susan: You are saying they already have a Friend Economy, they just may not be leveraging it very well, is that right?

Roch: First, yes, I think they do have a Friend Economy that they are not leveraging to its full potential. And in addition, I am encouraging them to create a very purposeful community around them. They have a group of people they know already and I'm encouraging them to be authentic and real about who they are. I encourage them to share who they are with this group. It's an easy way to start.

Second, I am encouraging them to create a larger community of their own. I want them to expand their community as they may only know a few dozen people now. You may need a thousand people to run your business profitably, so they need to look at not just tapping into the people they already know, but to start building a larger community around them.

Susan: When someone gets their Friend Economy working and in place, what happens? What results can they expect?

Roch: The first thing that comes to mind is when you have a group of people who really care about you and want to see you succeed. When they champion you and who you are personally helping, your self-confidence goes up. You feel better about what you are doing when you know the people you really love and trust aren't going to be taken advantage of by a competitor. It is a good feeling knowing if the economy turns bad again this group of people will stick with you until the very end, because they are friends. We have a different relationship than the typical business client relationship.

How Using The Friend Economy Means You Don't Have to Worry About Losing Clients

Susan: That's a key point you just made. A lot of business owners don't have this confidence, right? They have clients sure, but do they have confidence their clients would stick with them no matter what? I'm guessing a lot don't have this confidence.

Roch: Correct. I believe most business owners have a sense of, "I've got some trusted clients I think would be with me until the very end, but we always wonder if something changed, would they really be with me?" You know a friend will always be with you. You don't have to worry about losing clients like someone who doesn't have their Friend Economy in place.

The Friend Economy Works for All Personality Types

Susan: I'm curious Roch, have you always felt this way? Have you always been so passionate about helping others?

Roch: No. I was very socially awkward in high school and in college. I have always had a passion or a heart to help people, but I have not been as outgoing about it. I will be 50 years-old this year. I think as my business has grown and I have experienced life, I have gotten more comfortable in my own skin. This has been something that has evolved with me.

Susan: The reason I ask is, I wondered if certain personality styles have the inclination or their social compass points to being like this. For those of us who may not be as socially outgoing, would The Friend Economy still apply?

Roch: For someone who is not as outgoing, I would suggest it is even more important to build their Friend Economy. I consider myself an introvert. If I had my druthers and you asked me what I like to do to relax, my answer would be, I would not want to be in a room full of people having conversations. Some people are really good at working a room. I have conversations with people because I really want to make an impact in their lives. A week doesn't go by that I don't get two or three handwritten thank you cards or e-mails where people are acknowledging the impact that I have had on their lives.

Susan: It is hard for me to believe that you haven't always been this confident and outgoing.

Roch: If somebody is a little bit socially awkward or a little bit introverted, like myself, knowing their massive transformative purpose will help them become more outgoing. When you are really comfortable with what you stand for, you are not as timid about approaching people and having a conversation with them.

Don't Focus on Yourself, Focus on Your Clients

Susan: When you change the focus from me having to put myself out there...to me making a difference in someone's life...that is a huge shift. Then it becomes easy.

Roch: Yes, it is a huge shift. When the focus is about the other person, I can have a half-hour conversation with somebody and as soon as they say, "Well, tell me a little bit about yourself." I don't even know what to say when they ask those sorts of questions. I would rather shift the conversation back to them as opposed to having it be on me.

Susan: So you suggest getting really curious about the people around you.

Roch: That's exactly right. I don't even know if anybody really cares anything about me. They want to improve their life and I can help them do that because that is my massive transformative purpose.

Mistakes to Avoid While Building Your Friend Economy

Susan: What are some of the mistakes to watch out for when someone is starting to build their own Friend Economy?

Roch: There are two things I've seen happen. You can go overboard with sharing your massive transformative purpose. Let's say a chiropractor is passionate about alleviating human trafficking. It would be a mistake if from the moment you walked into the office, they had brochures, posters and pictures everywhere and they constantly pitched it so it was really in your face. I don't want the massive transformative purpose to be the first thing that hits you in the face.

I think it is a big mistake when somebody says, "I'm all in, this is a great idea" and then forgets about their business and makes it more about their social mission than it is about their business.

Another mistake one can make in their massive transformative purpose is projecting something too soft such as, "I really want to fix the potholes in my neighborhood." That would be a mistake where it would cause people to ask, "Really? That's all you're about? That's all the deeper person you are and you want me to refer all my friends?"

You have to really think through your massive transformative purpose to make sure you're going to have an impact on the world and then handle it in such a way that it's honorable and respectful to the cause.

Susan: Does your massive transformative purpose need to be what your business does, or can it be different?

Roch: I think it can be absolutely separate or different. One of the commitments I have made is to build up and develop leaders for the next 25 years. I made a 25-year commitment to helping solve major problems in the world by developing great leaders, and I have leadership conferences here on a weekly basis at my office.

People who have a common interest in changing the world; having an impact on the world and becoming better leaders, come to my conferences and to my office to learn from the speakers, books, and information I share. Being a better leader has nothing to do with financial planning, investment, insurance and taxes. Some of those people, because they know we have something great in common, say, "Oh, by the way, what do you do?" or "How can I get connected to what you do?" Some of those people become clients but not all of them, and I don't expect all of them to, but we're friends and they may refer me to somebody else that needs a financial adviser.

First and foremost, I do it for the right reason and that is to develop and build great leaders to solve problems. The secondary benefit is some of those people will become clients. To answer your question, no, I don't believe it has to have anything to do with what business you are in.

Susan: Interesting, because I thought your massive transformative purpose was sort of tied directly into what you do, but you're...

Roch: My massive transformative purpose is to help people enjoy a better life. That is a big umbrella. One of the ways I do that is how I make a living, which is helping people make great decisions about their money. Another way I help people enjoy a better life is helping them become really great leaders. The Tranel Financial Group offers a myriad of leadership and networking opportunities with no charge for the events. Obviously, when I do investments with people, there are natural charges and fees that are built into that, that's how I make a living but the other opportunities of growth and networking are free.

In helping people enjoy a better life, I can do it through the financial planning side, which is where I make a living. I can also do it through my position on a board of directors. I also do it through my leadership passion. I cast a pretty wide net, which can incorporate lots of areas of my life.

Susan: I can see where business owners put their time in and maybe they are enthusiastic about their work, but there isn't this overarching, as you call it, umbrella, which is your massive transformative purpose.

Roch: Right. If you are going to be my good friend, I want to make sure our relationship is more than one dimensional. A good friend has lots of different areas in their life, which are interesting. I think you want to have friends who are broad, diverse, and interesting. If somebody just talks about their work all the time, I am not going to want to pick up the phone and call them.

Susan: Right.

Roch: If I am going to pick up the phone and call you and you're going to tell me about a great vacation you took or something you did for your church or a mission trip, I would think, "Every time I talk to that guy, he is always up to something. He's got some great information to share. I want to get to know him more."

Susan: Versus only making it about what their business practice is or service they offer? This, as you said, makes the relationship one dimensional. If the chiropractor fixing your back only discusses your alignment and never asks about you and your life, and sends you on your way, it wouldn't take much to switch if another chiropractor came along. Right? There is nothing holding the relationship together.

Roch: That's right. Because then you are business acquaintances and you are not really friends. Business acquaintances talk about business and that's the expected conversation you would have. Friends ask how things are going, and you really are going to tell them how things are going. "My son just got in a car accident." "My wife just got diagnosed with this." You share things that matter to you with friends. If a business acquaintance asks, "How are you doing?" and you say, "Great" and leave it at that, you don't dive any deeper. In the Friend Economy, you know the people in your community and you really share with them. You are being real and authentic. And as a result you have a stronger, more, enriching relationship with them. Which would you rather have?

The Paradox: It's Easier to Engage with Your Clients as a Friend than as a Business Acquaintance

Susan: Is it easier to engage people this way? You would think it is harder, but I'm wondering if that is not the case.

Roch: Yes, exactly right. When you just have a business acquaintance or business relationship, once that conversation about business is over, you are struggling with, "What are we going to talk about next?" It can be a lot of work to have a conversation and keep it going and have the person think you are interesting or exciting or you have a life. But when they are your friend, you just easily share what is going on with your life. "My son got in a car accident." Then it is easy to have a conversation with a good friend as opposed to worrying about having a superficial conversation with a business acquaintance. You are right.

The answer is...it is easier to have a conversation with a good friend than it is with a business acquaintance. You think it would be harder because you are going deeper, but it is actually easier.

Susan: Can you share the distinction between someone who is friendly and someone who has the Friend Economy?

Roch: You have to be friendly, you have to be likeable, and you have to be respectable and respectful of others. That is a given. You are not even going to get into the conversation or get invited to the community for the first time to have a conversation unless you are friendly...unless you are a beacon of light...unless people are attracted to you in some way. If you are sitting at the church function and your head is down and there is no eye contact and you are not "friendly," no one is going to come over to talk to you.

If you're the person who has a group of people around you, talking and laughing, you can invite someone over who is not in the group. You say, "Hey, Tom, come on over, I'm telling the story about my kid and how he happened to get into a crazy car accident." You become friends through being friendly, but you need to be friendly first before you can become friends.

Susan: Making the decision you want involvement with the Friend Economy isn't enough. You have to actually, actively engage in the process?

Roch: That is correct.

Here's How to Get Started on Your Friend Economy

Susan: If someone wants to start their own Friend Economy, how can they begin to get started.

Roch: One of the most important things to creating your Friend Economy is, to continue to actively create more community in your life. When I first started out, I had a core group of friends I engaged with. However, I wanted to go beyond my group of friends and impact more people's lives. Because I had a passion for helping people and wanted to have a bigger impact on the world the first community I created was a great team around me. We then came up with different ways we could meet and interact with more people. Out of this passion The Tranel Movement was born, which consists of different groups we engage with throughout the month.

To make a big impact and help people live a better life, we knew we had to meet and interact with more people. For example, we created a networking group called Freedom One Networking, where business owners and professionals meet every Thursday morning from 7:15am to 8:30am. Freedom One Networking started a year ago with 15 people. Now we have over 80 who meet, interact, have fun, share energy, share insight, advice and wisdom with each other. It is an example of a community our team created because we wanted to reach a bigger audience. A couple of years ago I, nor the team was connected with any of the people who are in the group, and now we consider them friends.

Another example of how we actively create community is, every other Wednesday a group called "Leadership Won" meets. We are very excited about this community as it is a community of leaders who are shakers and movers in different industries. We meet and listen not only to world renowned leaders but also local leaders who talk on a specific topic, and then we have a conversation around it.

Another passion we have is to help not-for-profit organizations have more impact in the world. Our team created Rally Together for not-for-profits and business people to get together twice a month. Every other Wednesday Rally Together has a meeting for the not-for-profits to talk about best practices. How do not-for-profits get connected with businesses in the community? How do they recruit really great boards of directors? What are some of the successful ways they fund-raise? How can we all learn from each other? That is what Rally Together is all about.

Another community we created is called Praising Women, where team members at Tranel meet with women and talk about their faith and how it impacts their role in the home, workplace, community and the world. This group meets once a month to discuss specific topics and issues and how they desire to grow and have an impact with their friends, family and workplaces.

We also have a few men's groups who get together as well. We have a Toastmasters group which meets every other Monday night. Through The Tranel Movement we have created communities, which otherwise would not exist, of people who have common interests. Our desire at The Tranel Financial

Group is to provide communities of common interest that people can be a part of to share, learn and grow as individuals. If they have an interest in any of them they can join. If they discover the group does not share their values, is not their style or simply not a fit for them they can find other opportunities for community.

The Tranel Movement has evolved from a desire to connect neighbors, friends and employees in order to grow, support and learn from one another.

Susan: For someone who is just hearing about The Friend Economy for the first time, would you suggest, Roch, they go out and start a new community or tap into an existing one?

Roch: I think they should start softly with the people they already know. If you have a group of 10 friends, I would have a conversation with each of them and say, "I want to tell you about this transformation I have had about who I am and what I stand for, and I want to share it with you. You are a close friend and I want to get some feedback. What are your thoughts?" Start your Friend Economy with the people you already know. Then as you get more comfortable, I would get a group of people together who have a common interest around your massive transformative purpose and start to have some really good conversations around it at a restaurant or a community center in your area. Or find a local company who will donate a conference room for you to use. I would start right away. If you are passionate about trying to transform the world, there's no better time than right now to start to have a conversation with great like-minded people. Don't wait.

Susan: How can someone who wants to tap into a community, which already exists similar to The Tranel Movement, find one?

Roch: Google.

Susan: Okay.

Roch: I think what will happen is that when you talk to your close friends and you tell them you are really passionate about changing the world in a certain way, they are going to respond. They will say, "Hey, at my church or at my community center on Thursdays they have something you should check out." I think you will be naturally connected with those groups through the people that you authentically share your passion with. In addition, I would continue to do research through the internet to see where some existing groups might be meeting, and go out on a limb and visit them, or reach out to whomever might be leading those groups.

Why Your Clients Are Happier When You Have a Friend Economy

Susan: Do your clients embrace this Roch?

Roch: Yes. They really like that I am passionate about helping people. Who wouldn't, right? They like the passion I bring. They like to hear my stories about how I have helped someone. Sometimes you can get as much enjoyment out of somebody telling you about a great vacation they recently had, than if you took the vacation yourself. I think my clients get behind me because they enjoy being around somebody who is a beacon of hope and optimism and has a mindset of anything is possible. They tell me they find it refreshing and they like to hear the different stories.

They know helping people is important to me and I enjoy hearing a story they have to share. Before I switched to my Friend Economy, our conversations would just have been talking about money issues. Now we are still talking about serious financial issues, but they share with me stories about how they have gotten on board with my passion and mission to help others and share those types of stories. There is a lot more enthusiasm to the relationship now that we relate as friends versus just as adviser to client.

Susan: It seems like it is more comprehensive. You have a much deeper relationship with your clients than the average financial planner or CPA who just sits down doing your taxes or what have you. Seems like your clients would appreciate that you truly care about them and what they are up to.

Roch: They certainly do and because I have become friends with them, they let me into areas of their lives they otherwise would not have. And because of that, I can help them solve other problems or have conversations about concerns they have that another adviser would not get a chance to. The great benefit to going to this deeper level is that I am actually able to be a better adviser to them. If you are a doctor in the medical profession, and a patient were to share some deep concerns about something, it may help you as a doctor, to treat them better than if they did not feel comfortable sharing it. It helps me as an adviser to be friends with my clientele. There is no question.

How to Join and Be a Part of Roch's Friend Economy

Susan: Where can someone go if they want to join your community? Or to see how you have setup your Friend Economy?

Roch: If they go to TranelMovement.com they can see the events we have going on. They can see if they would like to come and be involved in our movement and the impact we're having on the world. Or they can say, "Those passions are not interesting to me, but I would like to come and see how they run their events so I can learn how to start my own movement or my own community." They can learn from the different types of communities The Tranel Financial Group has put together.

Susan: Your entire organization model is the Friend Economy model, correct?

Roch: Correct, absolutely correct.

Susan: If someone has questions about starting their own Friend Economy or if they want more information how can they be in touch, Roch?

Roch: I think the best way to reach me is the same way you would reach out to a good friend. You pick up the phone and call. They can go to TranelMovement.com and get a sense of what we're all about. But I would encourage people to pick up the phone and call me at 847-680-9050. Just pick up the phone and give me a call and ask me a question about The Friend Economy; about my passion for helping people enjoy a better life and how to really get connected. I will tell them how to get into my community, and I will share how I can help them build their community.

Susan: That's a really refreshing approach, Roch. A lot of people are hesitant to say, "Pick up the phone and call me." We may be putting up a barrier when we automatically point people to sign up for our newsletter to learn more. You're saying if we are going to be friends, I need to walk my talk and say call me. That's pretty refreshing in today's busy rush around world.

Roch: Friends call friends.

Susan: You make a good point. If you have not been connecting with your clients, pick up the phone and ask, "How are you doing?"

Roch: It would blow some people away.

Susan: Agreed, and such a simple thing to do. Any final thoughts?

Roch: I am encouraged with the impact this book could have on someone's business and the impact it could have on the world. To have people feel really comfortable with who they are, communicating that to the world around them and their community. And, then going even further and starting new communities around topics they are passionate about. The possibilities are limitless. This will have a tremendous impact on people's lives for the better. I am walking proof of that. Our communities are proof of that as well. We are excited to see the results.

Susan: It is interesting because a lot of business owners may assume they have this in place, but they have not taken it to the level you are suggesting here. I encourage everyone who is reading this to stop and really take a look at their Friend Economy. My sense is, people are not embracing this but think they are, because they post on Facebook, Twitter and LinkedIn. You are painting a much bigger game for them.

Roch: Correct, that's exactly right. You are formalizing your community to where you have a way of meeting on a periodic basis. I've organized my community so we have a way to get together and a reason and a purpose to get together. We have a structure for when we do get together on how we are going to act and conduct ourselves.

Susan: These communities are for the benefit of your community or Friend Economy, not just for the benefit of you. You are providing values so they want to come and be a part of something greater than themselves. As you said, if we have another downturn in the economy, you will have confidence your clients are not going to jump ship at the first sign of a problem, because they are more than just clients to you, they are your friends.

Roch: That is exactly right. I am very grateful for this opportunity to expand someone's thinking around this area, because it can make a very meaningful difference in their lives and the lives of their friends.

Susan: Thank you, Roch, it has been very enlightening for me too.

Here's How to Build an Abundant Business Powered by a Community of Friends

Let's face it, having to focus on both attracting new business and reaching your next wave of clients is exhausting!

That is where The Friend Economy comes into play. The Friend Economy helps business owners just like you create a thriving community of friends who want to do business with you, which stops the cycle of client chasing once and for all.

Here are three ways to get started building your Friend Economy today.

Step 1: Come to our next Freedom One Networking Group to see Roch's Friend Economy in action. Visit: http://www.thefriendeconomy.com for more information.

Step 2: Form your own Friend Economy by bringing together a small community of friends and colleagues around a common interest. Start by scheduling monthly meetings with you as the leader. For more ideas on how to grow your Friend Economy go to TranelMovement.com.

Step 3: Call or email Roch and share your Friend Economy idea with him and ask him any questions you have about how to start your Friend Economy.

847-680-9050 | roch@thefriendeconomy.com

Now you can ensure your business will grow even when times are tough. When you incorporate the Friend Economy into your life, you will never have to worry about growing your business again. After all, what are friends for!

About the Author

Roch Tranel, Certified Financial Planner, is president and founder of The Tranel Financial Group located in Libertyville, Illinois. Roch has been helping individuals reach clarity and confidence about their financial future for over 25 years. Helping people *Enjoy a Better Life* through successful financial planning is Roch's passion in life. Roch has assembled a team of professional financial advisors who are committed to the same principles and share the same commitment to providing unparalleled client experience.

As an active leader in his community, Roch has served on several boards which include the GLMV Chamber, The Rotary Club, Great Lakes Adaptive Sports Association and The National Christian Foundation of Greater Chicago. Roch is also very passionate and active in growing The Tranel Movement which includes leadership, community growth and networking opportunities.

Roch resides in Libertyville, Illinois, with his wife, Kathleen and their children Jenna and Alec.

The Friend Economy has been a continuing theme in Roch's career since his first days as a Certified Financial Planner to the present as a leader, mentor and friend. Building a community of friends around himself has allowed Roch to enjoy a rich and rewarding career and life. Roch is committed to using his massive transformative purpose to create communities that inspire others toward being great leaders in their home, community and the world.

The
TRANEL
Financial Group

roch@thefriendeconomy.com
1509 N. Milwaukee Avenue, Libertyville, Illinois,
60048 | Office: 847-680-9050 | Fax: 847-680-9051
www.TranelFinancial.com

*Introductions to your family, friends and associates
are the highest compliments we receive.*

*Committed to helping clients achieve
Clarity & Confidence...*

Helping people Enjoy A Better Life™ since 1988!